The m&m's® BRAND

Addition Book

$$1 + 1 = 2$$

Barbara Barbieri McGrath

Charlesbridge

Love to my brother Al, who helps make things add up!

—B. B. M.

Text copyright © 2004 by Barbara Barbieri McGrath
Illustrations copyright © 2004 by Charlesbridge Publishing
All rights reserved, including the right of reproduction in whole or in part in any form.
Charlesbridge and colophon are registered trademarks of Charlesbridge Publishing, Inc.

Published by Charlesbridge
85 Main Street
Watertown, MA 02472
(617) 926-0329
www.charlesbridge.com

Library of Congress Cataloging-in-Publication Data
McGrath, Barbara Barbieri, 1954–
    The M&M'S® Brand addition book / Barbara Barbieri McGrath.
        p. cm.
    Summary: Rhyming text and illustrations use candy to teach mathematical skills, including
review of counting and estimation and single- and double-digit addition.
    ISBN 0-88106-348-7 (reinforced for library use)
    ISBN 0-88106-349-5 (softcover)
1. Addition—Juvenile literature. [1. Addition.] I. Title: M&M'S® Brand addition book. II. Title.
QA115.M387 2004
513.2'11—dc22   2003015902

Printed in Korea
(hc) 10 9 8 7 6 5 4 3 2 1
(sc) 10 9 8 7 6 5 4 3 2 1

Display type set in Hip Hop and text type set in Adobe Caslon
Printed and bound by Sung In Printing, South Korea
Production supervision by Brian G. Walker
Designed by Susan Mallory Sherman

™/® & © M&M'S, M and the M&M'S Characters are trademarks of Mars, Incorporated and its affiliates.
© Mars, Inc. Manufactured and distributed under license by Charlesbridge Publishing.

Look at the bag. It's where M&M'S® hide.
Can you guess how many M&M'S® are inside?

Guessing how many M&M'S® Chocolate Candies are
in a bag is fun because there is no wrong answer.
This is called estimating.

To get an answer about the amount,
Pour out the candies and count, count, count!

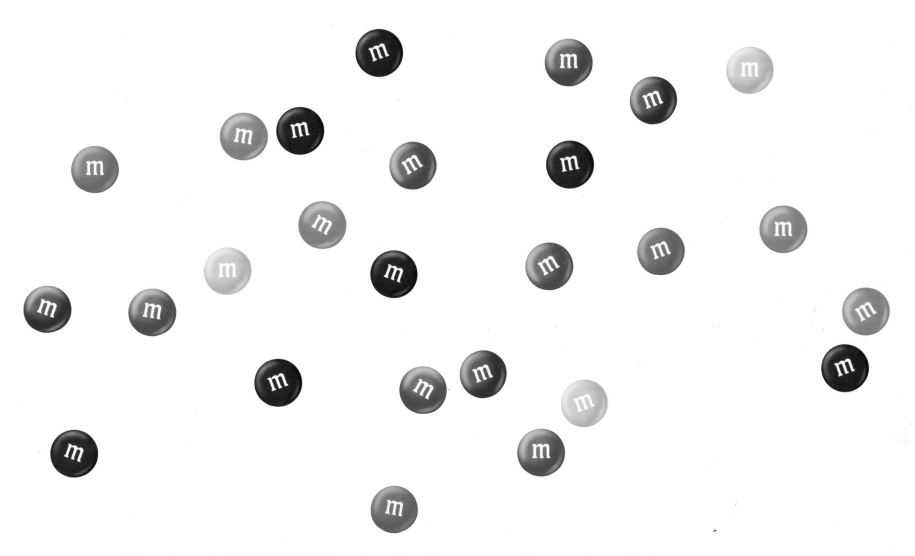

Counting the M&M'S® Chocolate Candies means giving each candy its own number name. This could take a while! There are usually about 50 M&M'S® Chocolate Candies in a small bag.

Sort them by color. Call each group a set.
Count each different color, but don't eat them yet!

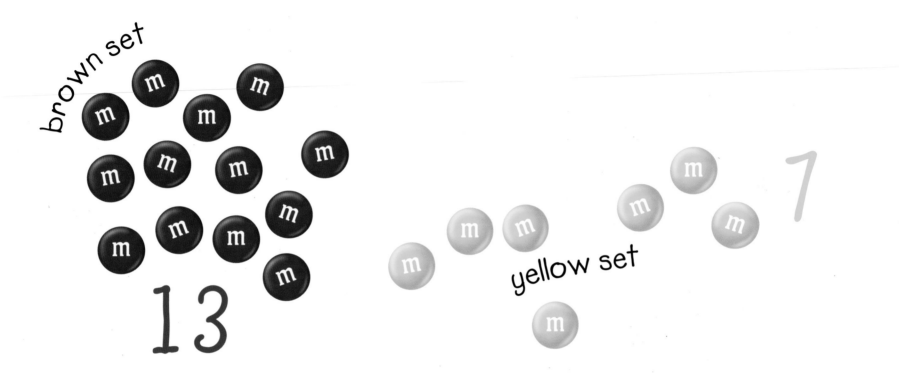

brown set

13

yellow set

7

Sorting gets things organized. Sorting objects can be done
in many ways. Here we are sorting M&M'S® Chocolate
Candies by color. Just by looking at each color group,
you can probably tell which color has the most M&M'S®
Chocolate Candies. Count the M&M'S® Chocolate Candies
in each set and write that number down.

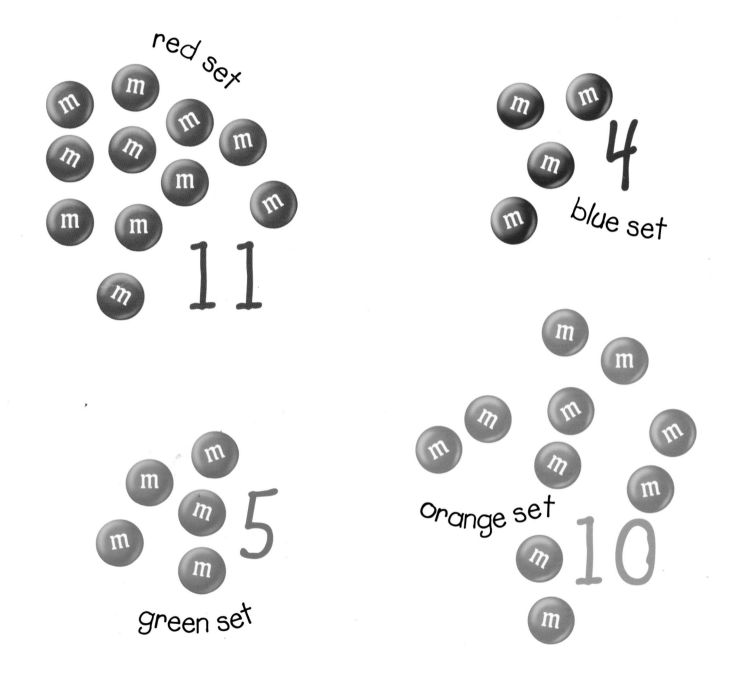

red set

11

blue set

4

green set

5

orange set

10

When you want to have more, add to get a sum.

Combine two groups together. The total is—yum!

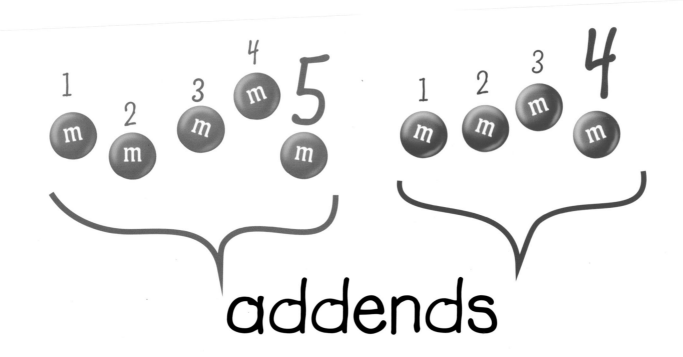

The numbers you add are called addends.

There are five green and four blue M&M'S® Chocolate Candies.
When you put the two colors together and then count them,
there will be nine M&M'S® Chocolate Candies.

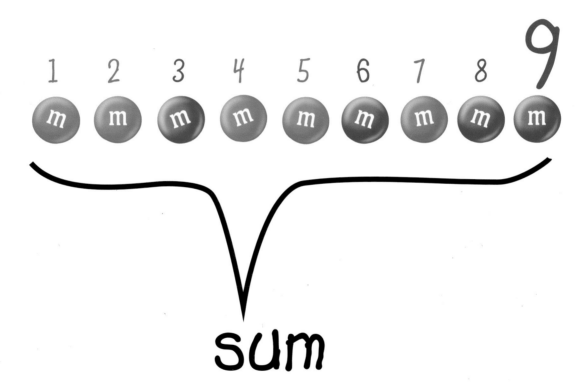

The total is called the sum.

Let's write an equation, then turn it around.

The numbers aren't dizzy, and the sum is still found.

An equation is a number sentence. The equation you just did looks like this:

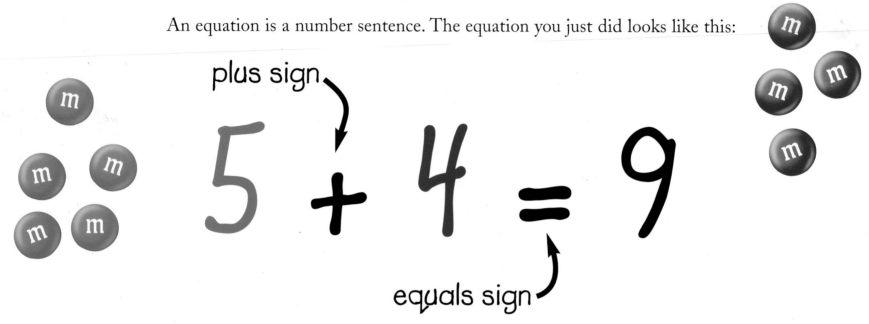

plus sign

equals sign

The plus sign means add. It goes between the two numbers you want to add.

The numbers on each side of the equals sign must have the same value.

Equations can also be reversed, like this:

$$4 + 5 = 9$$

Look at this equation. Does it look rather tall?
Addition can be vertical—it's no trouble at all!

You can also write the numbers one on top of the other, like this:

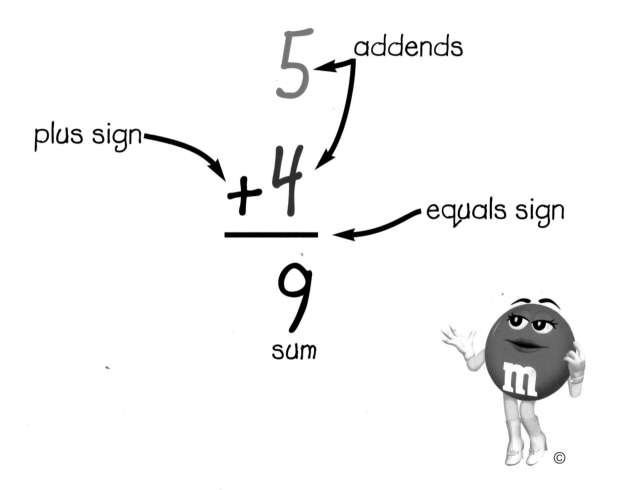

addends

plus sign

equals sign

sum

No matter how you do it, the answer is definitely 9!

All numbers have value, a fact we must face.

See them in columns. Put them in their place.

The numbers 0 through 9 are called digits.

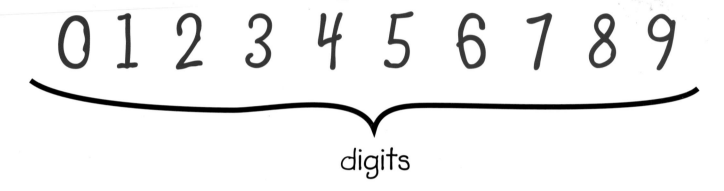

digits

Bigger numbers, from 10 to 99, use two digits:

one digit in the ones column and one digit in the tens column.

tens column

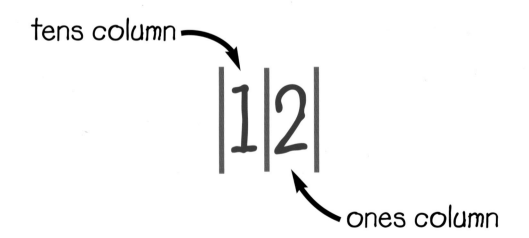

ones column

12

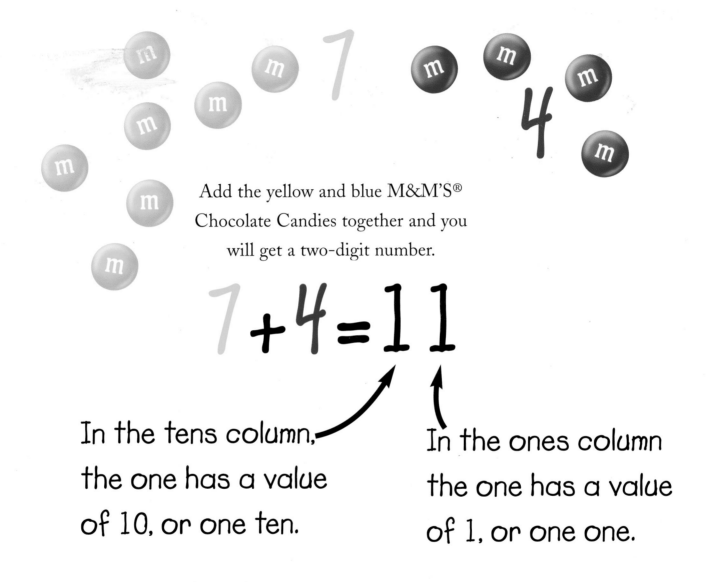

Add the yellow and blue M&M'S® Chocolate Candies together and you will get a two-digit number.

$7 + 4 = 11$

In the tens column, the one has a value of 10, or one ten.

In the ones column the one has a value of 1, or one one.

Digits can have different values depending on their place in the number.

Red plus green, yellow plus green, and orange plus blue,
Let's practice adding. Each sum will be new.

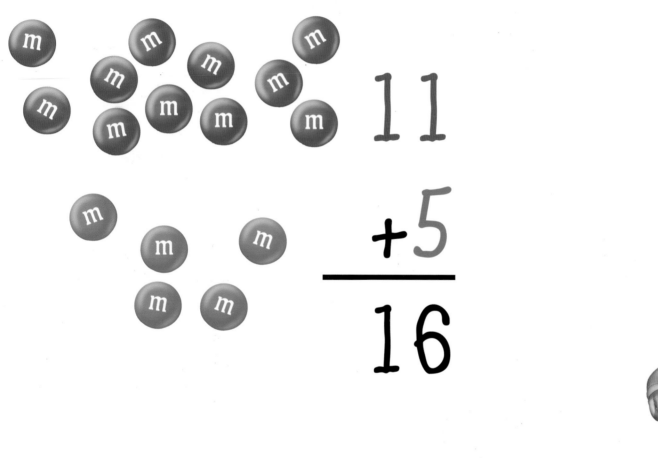

$$\begin{array}{r} 11 \\ +5 \\ \hline 16 \end{array}$$

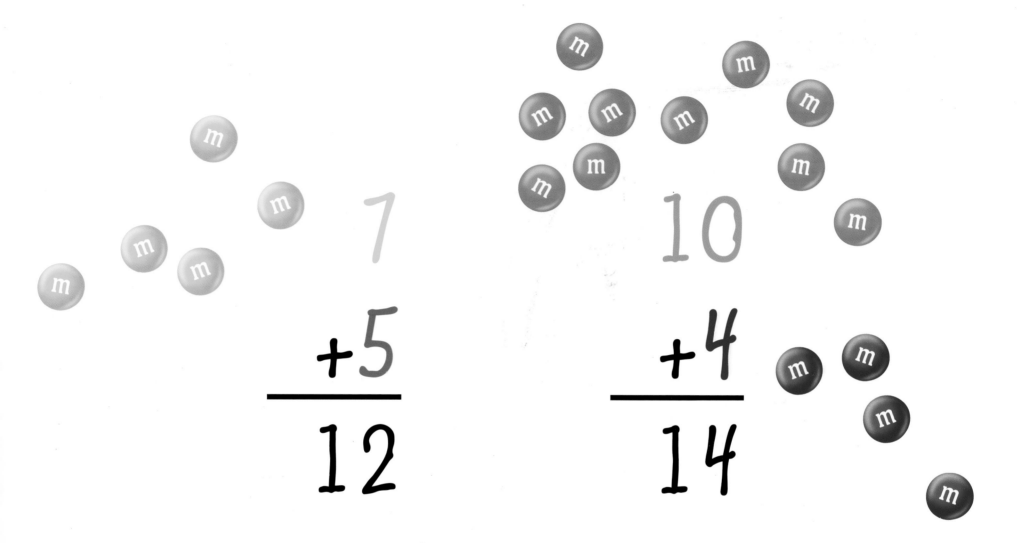

7
+5
―――
12

10
+4
―――
14

15

Adding two-digit numbers will mean even more.
Bigger and bigger, the numbers will soar!

Watch what happens when we add the orange and red M&M'S® Chocolate
Candies together.

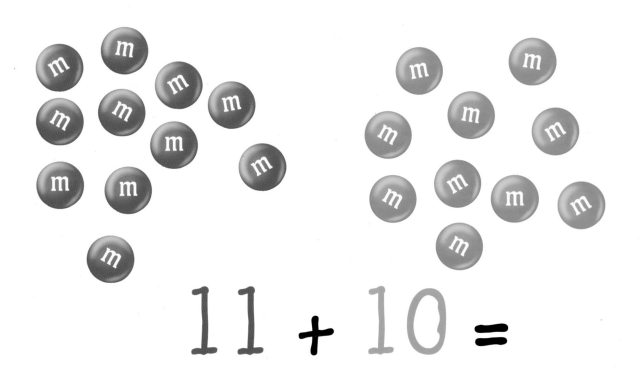

11 + 10 =

When you add double-digit numbers, it's easier to add vertically.

tens column   ones column

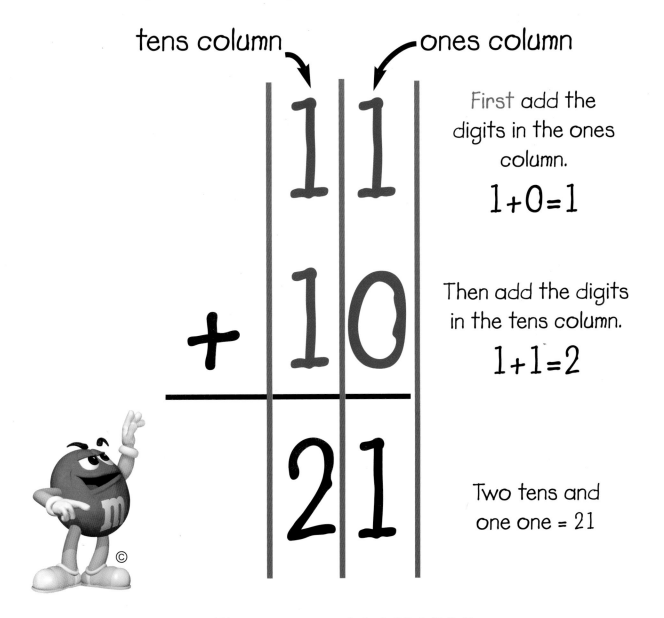

First add the digits in the ones column.
1+0=1

Then add the digits in the tens column.
1+1=2

Two tens and one one = 21

There are 21 M&M'S®
Chocolate Candies total.

Orange plus brown, red plus blue—write it down.

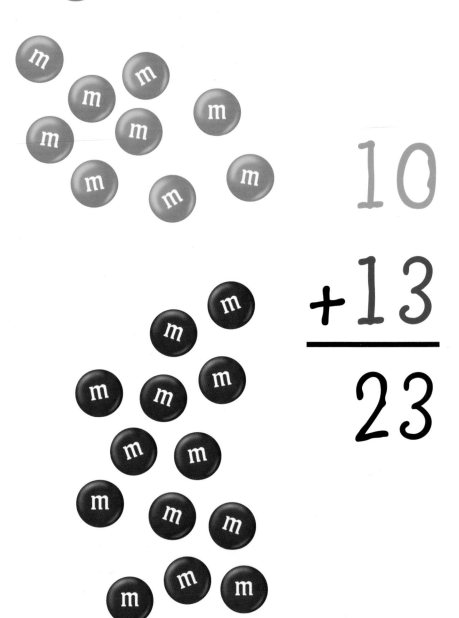

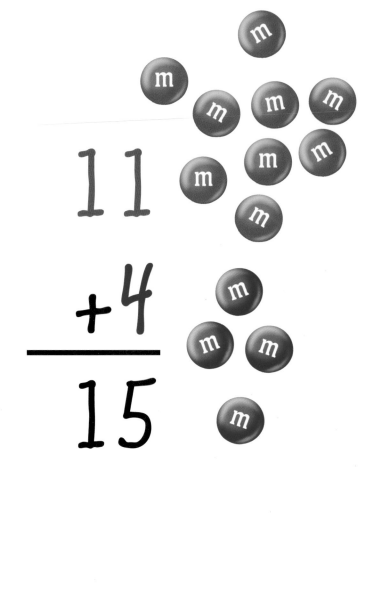

$$10$$
$$+13$$
$$\overline{23}$$

$$11$$
$$+4$$
$$\overline{15}$$

18

Add the sums: red and blue plus orange and brown.

$$15$$
$$+23$$
$$\overline{}$$
$$38$$

To add bigger numbers, take a breath, don't get tense—
You'll need to carry or it just won't make sense!

Let's add all the color sets together. Set up your number columns.

m Add the numbers in the ones column.

They add up to 20. That simply doesn't fit!

The 2 in 20 must get over to the tens column.

m Carry the 2 and place it in the tens column.

The tens column has 3 tens already.

m Add the numbers in the tens column.

There are 5 tens total.

So the answer is 50.

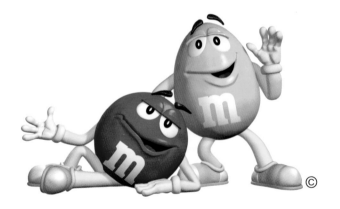

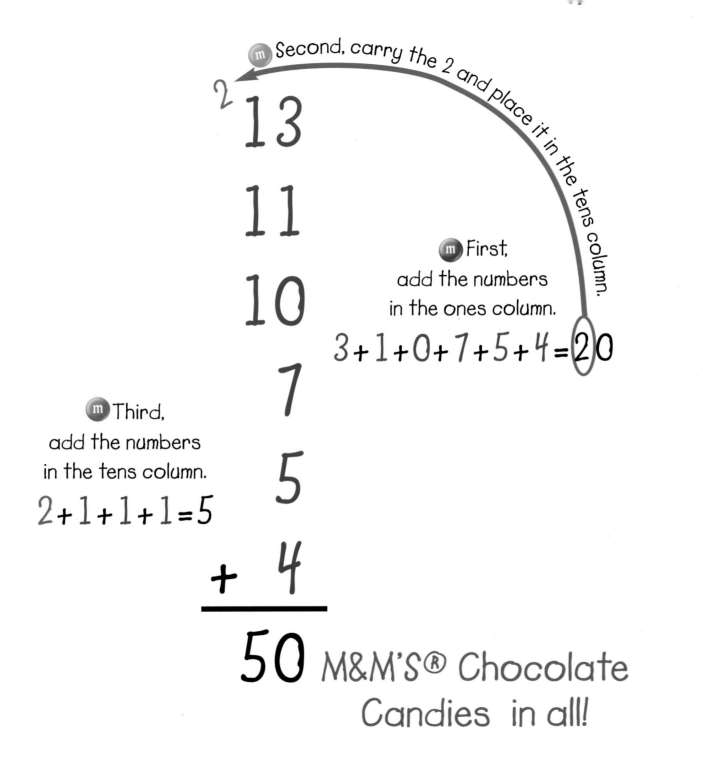

Second, carry the 2 and place it in the tens column.

$$2$$
$$13$$
$$11$$
$$10$$
$$7$$
$$5$$
$$+ \ 4$$
$$\overline{}$$
$$50$$

First, add the numbers in the ones column.

$$3+1+0+7+5+4=20$$

Third, add the numbers in the tens column.

$$2+1+1+1=5$$

50 M&M'S® Chocolate Candies in all!

Addition was fun, but there is a way

The M&M'S® in the bag can be taken away.

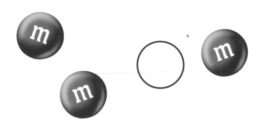

It's called subtraction!

In addition you add to get a sum. Adding M&M'S® Chocolate Candies is great because you get more. In subtraction you take away to find the difference. Subtracting is even better because you get to make M&M'S® Chocolate Candies disappear! Eat one of each color. This is a great way to end an addition book.

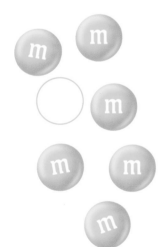

22

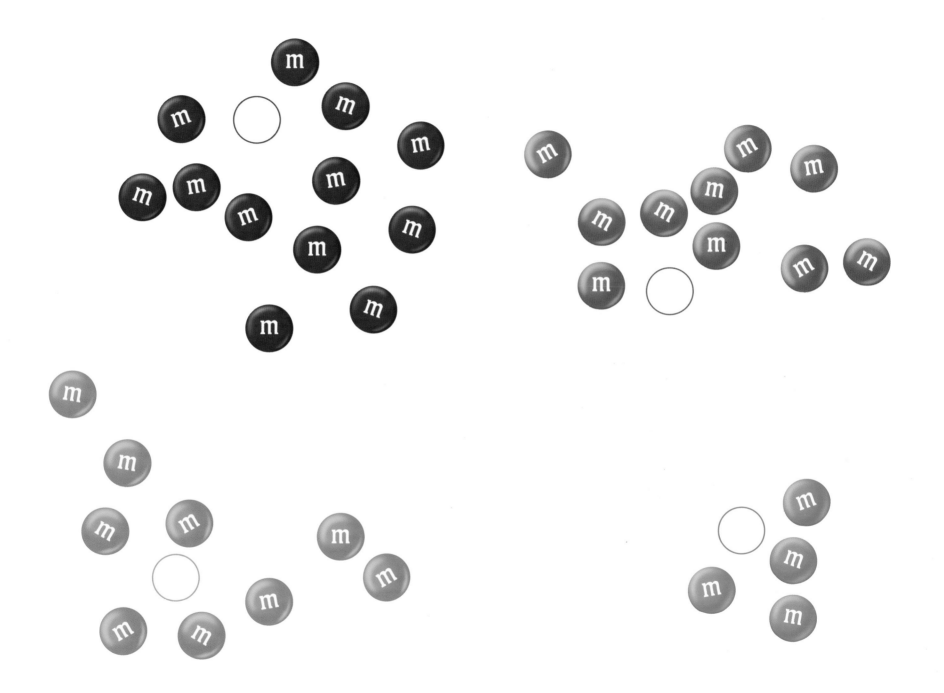

You've done M&M'S® addition. That sure was a lot!
A review helps to remember—it's more food for thought.

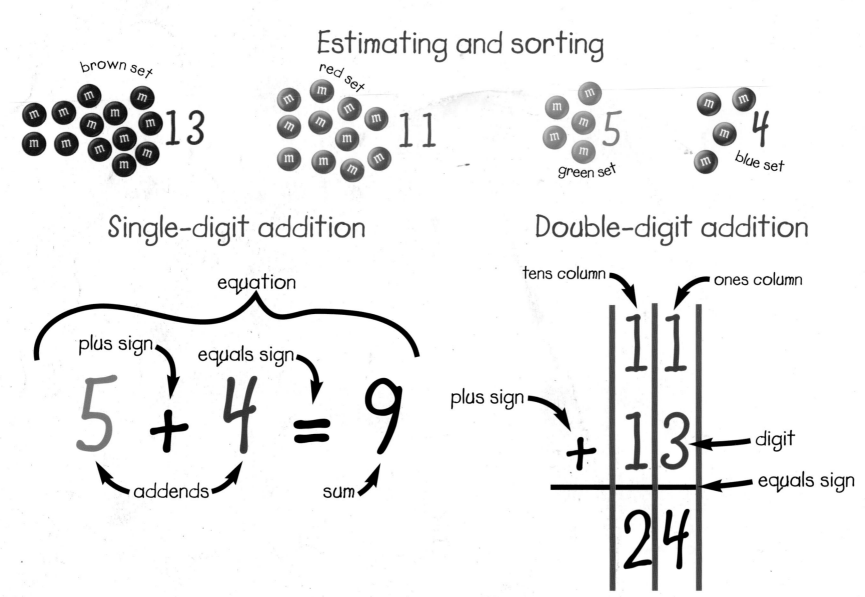

Estimating and sorting

brown set 13

red set 11

green set 5

blue set 4

Single-digit addition

equation

plus sign
equals sign

5 + 4 = 9

addends
sum

Double-digit addition

tens column   ones column

plus sign

```
  1 1
+ 1 3
-------    digit
  2 4      equals sign
```